QUEST FOR QUALITY IN THE CHURCH

A NEW PARADIGM

EZRA EARL JONES
General Secretary
General Board of Discipleship

DISCIPLESHIP RESOURCES
MATERIALS FOR GROWTH IN CHRISTIAN FAITH & LIFE
NASHVILLE, TENNESSEE

❖ **TO PLACE AN ORDER** or to Inquire About Resources and Customer Accounts, Contact:

Discipleship Resources Distribution Center
P.O. Box 6996
Alpharetta, Georgia 30239-6996

Tel: (800) 685-4370

Fax: (404) 442-5114

❖ **FOR EDITORIAL INQUIRIES** and Rights and Permissions Requests, Contact:

Discipleship Resources Editorial Offices
P.O. Box 840
Nashville, Tennessee 37202-0840

Tel: (615) 340-7068

Cover design by Tim Hornbeak.

Text illustrations by Mary S. Jones.

Library of Congress Catalog Card No. 93-72756

ISBN 0-88177-129-5

DR129

Contents

> *Basic assumptions of our day — competition, short-term profits, quick results, and individualistic values — tend to block our ability to see the merits of a philosophy of leadership that is based on very different values — values of cooperation, long-term and continual improvement, and team work.*

Introduction

Total Quality Improvement (Quest for Quality) — a phrase describing a view of work, people, and how they interact — is a fairly new concept to most North Americans. Even as recently as fifteen years ago, few people in the United States were familiar with the phrase. The concept may be traced to its introduction into Japanese business culture following World War II. Some of its main tenets, however, were developed much earlier in the century by Walter A. Shewart, W. Edwards Deming, Joseph M. Juran, and others.

To the uninitiated, quality improvement theory may appear to be just one more management scheme. Journalists and business analysts, in their continuing search for stories, are already suggesting that the benefits of quality improvement are limited to just a few companies and organizations and that quality improvement has failed in many settings. Basic assumptions of our day — competition, short-term profits, quick results, and individualistic values — tend to block our ability to see the merits of a philosophy of leadership that is based on very different values — values of cooperation, long-term and continual improvement, and team work.

Quality improvement theory (or Quest for Quality, as we call it in the church) has assumptions and characteristics that are different from the prevailing cultural norms.

Quest for Quality is a *total operating perspective and framework*, not a program.

It is *"breakthrough thinking,"* not "the same old way."

It is a *structured, disciplined approach* to identifying processes that are not working well; improving the processes; then standardizing and further improving the advancements made. It is not firefighting.

It is *long-term*; not short-term.

It is a *permanent way of living together* in the organization. It is not a "quick fix."

As a leader and advisor of leaders in the church for more than three decades, by the age of fifty, I had become quite skilled in pushing myself and others to work harder, certain that we were just around the corner to finding the panacea for the problems of mainline churches. For some reason (not based upon any data), I was sure that, with the "right solution," we would move forward together to build the City of God.

One day a friend made this simple statement: "The system is designed for the results it is getting. If you want different results, you will have to redesign the system."

> The system is designed for the results it is getting. If you want different results, you will have to redesign the system.

That statement changed my life. It changed the way I live, lead, manage, and act. I have learned to think differently and to pursue different kinds of knowledge. Drawn by that statement's simple truth, my colleagues in the General Board of Discipleship and I have embarked on a new journey toward quality. Our journey involves listening at new levels to our people. Our journey is one of continuous improvement.

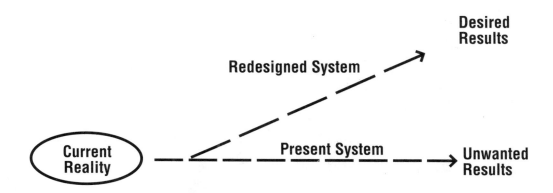

We believe that this simple insight can help us change and rebuild the ministry of our church. We can redesign our systems, but first we must clarify what aim we want. When we are clear and confident of our aim, we can appropriately design an organization and a way of operating to produce that aim. We must also learn new ways of leading the redesigned systems.

The simple insight about designing systems appropriate to desired results is working in all sorts of organizations outside the church. Those learnings don't tell us how to operate in the church, but they do give us some knowledge to build on. We have heard again and again that improvement and change follow clarity of visions. It is true. Moreover, improvement and change require that systems be designed around those visions. Improvement and change are dependent also upon leaders with the ability to listen and to change themselves.

Quest for Quality is not for everyone. Some are "succeeding" to their satisfaction in old ways of thinking. Some believe it is too painful or difficult to change. Some are suspicious of bringing any insights into the church that did not originate in the church or that cannot be put into church language.

> Quest for Quality is not for everyone. Some are "succeeding" to their satisfaction in old ways of thinking. Some believe it is too painful or difficult to change.

Still others view the church as a mystical community of saints and downplay the church's role as a primary social institution. Some will find it impossible to assign the church's past failures to a system rather than to people, leaders, theology, or some sinister conspiracy (liberalism, fundamentalism, communism, or the like). Personally, I still find it is easier to blame others than to figure out how to improve the system.

> Personally, I still find it is easier to blame others than to figure out how to improve the system.

On the other hand, it is freeing to discover that the failure of my efforts to produce better results for the church may not be due to my theology and vision or my leadership abilities. There is another possibility: The system I built (or inherited) may not be capable of producing the vision. Moreover, the system can't be overridden by the force of leadership and activity. I do need to work on the vision, but I need a system that values the process of visioning and empowers it. I do need to work on leadership, but I need a system that grounds leadership theory in the practice of managing a particular system to achieve a particular vision. It is possible to work on vision, system, and leadership at the same time.

> The system can't be overridden by the force of leadership and activity.

Our present systems in The United Methodist Church and in other mainline denominations were not designed to function as they do. Over many years — generations even — processes have slowly changed as the systems "settled" and adjusted to the world around them. In some cases, we have tampered with processes to solve immediate problems, totally unaware that, in a system, every small adjustment may issue in multiple small and large quivers and changes elsewhere in the system.

In many ways, our present systems look the same as they always have — but looks are deceiving. The systems function differently. Some processes are now disconnected from the basic workings of the system and do not add value. They channel our efforts and energies into vacuums. Sometimes processes that once produced value for the ministry system now do harm to the system. They are connected to other parts and processes in ways that diminish their value.

The other possibility (and often an inevitability) is that processes that are still valid are reduced in significance because the primary core processes of the ministry system that they are designed to support are in disarray or are dysfunctional. Ministry takes place fundamentally in the interactions between congregations and the people in the communities they serve. Congregations are supported in this by conferences and general church structures. If these fundamental relationships are malfunctioning, supplemental support programs that provide curriculum materials, training, skill development, and the like (even though these may be of the highest quality) have little or no effect. The temptation is to keep using programs and methods that enhanced the church's ministry when the basic processes were functioning — as though these programs and methods can substitute for the basic interactions linking people to the work of the church or as though they can somehow heal or fix the primary processes. Some of us have so identified programs for *supporting* or *enhancing* ministry with ministry itself (the process of people assisting one another in Christian faith development) that we do not distinguish ends from means.

> Some of us have so identified programs for **supporting** or **enhancing** ministry with ministry itself (the process of people assisting one another in Christian faith development) that we do not distinguish ends from means.

Quest for Quality is a viable pathway for God's radical transformation through Christ of the church and other institutions. It is a stance, a principle, a framework.

- It is open to change; in fact, it demands change.

- It insists on clarity of mission and vision. "Where there is no vision, the people perish" (Proverbs 29:18, KJV).

- While we religious professionals are focusing on the cosmic answers, Quest for Quality asks the people about their lives, their yearnings, their search for God, and their experiences of God.

- The goal of Quest for Quality is to remind us that a person, a church, or any organization is a creation, fearfully and wonderfully made. Those who are made stewards of the church are to take care of it and improve it.

- Quest is open to the continuing revelation of God and the particulars of specific social settings.

I have purposely tried to keep this book brief. It is a primer, rather than a systematic treatment. The first several chapters outline the rudiments of Quest for Quality and clarify the meaning of the term *quality*, who judges it (the customer*), and who defines it (the producer).

Succeeding chapters address mission and vision, systems and processes, and leadership. The core process or primary task of the organization is discussed at greater length.

Quest for Quality is a systems approach to the work of the church. It is a recognition that all parts and processes contribute to the whole, to a common aim, and to interdependence in functions.

Quality itself is systemic. A quality church that produces quality in outreach, worship, nurture, and ministry:

- Is clear about its mission. It is motivated by a compelling vision of transcendent worship and neighborly caring.

- Pays attention to all the parts and processes that make up the organizational system and relates those parts appropriately.

---

*Quality Improvement has developed its own vocabulary, which is used by leaders and practitioners in all fields — profit and nonprofit, manufacturing and service organizations. Included are such terms as *customer, supplier, variation, optimization,* and others. It is important that we in the church do not allow these business and marketing terms to influence negatively our appropriation of quality improvement in the church.

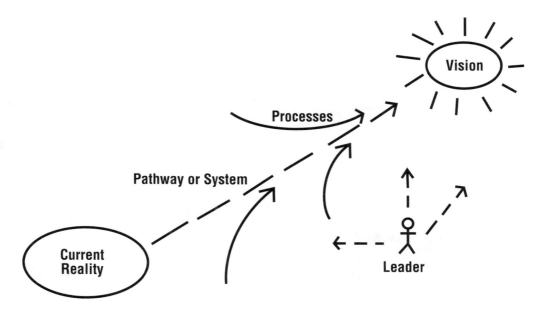

- Leads the church to produce the vision even as it continually pushes out the visions of new possibilities.

If you are a part of one of these churches, you know the excitement and wonder of it all. The pages that follow are intended to make quality possible in every community.

Acknowledgments

Cheryl Capshaw helped me rewrite and edit this book.

Mary Jones created the text graphics.

Janice Grana, Alan Waltz, and Victor Pérez-Silvestry
read and reacted to the first draft.

The thinking of our teachers
Ed Deming, Paul Batalden, and Susan Hillenmeyer
are found on every page.

Scores of others in the General Board of Discipleship
and the church contributed too.

> *Quest is a distinctive view of the work of the church, people, and how the two intersect.*

CHAPTER 1

A New Alternative

P eople live out their lives in all sorts of ways. They live as individuals, in some measure independent of others. But they also live interdependently as members of families and communities.

One of the many places people spend time is the church. In the United States, for most of the twentieth century, church membership and participation have varied little. Seven out of ten people in the United States claim membership in a religious institution, and four out of those seven attend worship each week.

Why do people go to church? There are many reasons. Perhaps underlying the varied reasons people attend church is a yearning to be in touch with God — with the one who created the world and gave us life.

People need assurance that God is with them, just as a child needs to know that Mother or Father is there, is watching, and is dependable.

As people seek and find God in many places in their lives, as they go to church to find God or to celebrate God's goodness and greatness, they go both as individuals and as members of a community —

- ◆ The community where they live;
- ◆ Their peer community (students, friends, business associates);
- ◆ The family community;
- ◆ The church community.

Interdependence is both a sociological phenomenon (people relating in society) and a theological event (people finding God with and through one another and learning to live together as caring neighbors).

People usually participate in the church through attendance in worship services, through caring or nurture groups such as Sunday school, through social activities, and through outreach and service to others.

Much goes into creating, designing, planning, and carrying out church activities. The ordained clergy, the lay leaders, and all participants provide valuable leadership and talent for the good of the whole.

The most visible and generally best-attended church activity — the worship service — usually includes sermons, prayers, litanies, Scripture readings, musicians, choirs, acolytes, lay readers, and much more. The church school offers classrooms, lessons, curriculum materials, teachers, discussions, and (maybe) picnics. In the church, there are sacraments, confirmations, weddings, funerals, ordinations, musicals and dramas, retreats, and times of silence.

As with any institution's (school, business, hospital, or club) services, church services may be pleasing and attractive, or they may be unpleasant or boring. Further, what pleases some may displease others.

How do we know? How can we design church activities that deal with the needs of all who come or may come, given the diversity of needs, desires, and expectations people bring?

How might your church provide *more* than people expect? How might your church surprise and delight participants? How might your church provide experiences of depth that are life-changing, that bring people into the presence of God? How might your church nurture the religious community so they become living ambassadors for Christ wherever they go?

How might your church be a missionary congregation, inviting persons to join in the lifelong Christian journey?

How might your church be a major force in the community for creating a loving and just world?

It is possible for your church to serve and to extend its ministry to others better than ever before. You don't need a complicated planning process, but you have to do some basic things:

1. Listen to people's deepest yearnings.
2. Put together a system that will meet people's basic expectations of the church.
3. Improve that system so that it goes beyond people's expectations to delight and excite them.
4. Act — through leaders — to empower all the people to contribute to the effort.

Our subject is quality! We are talking about what congregations need to do to satisfy people's deepest religious needs. We want to challenge those who design, plan, and carry out the functions of the church to envision levels of quality in church life that may go beyond their own experience.

We do not want to glorify short-range solutions or gimmicks. We are not suggesting that your church should compete more with other churches. We simply want to suggest that your church can improve its ministries. You can create settings in your church that will attract people because those settings are worshipful, nurturing, or inviting; or because they open opportunities for meaningful service. It is possible for you to continue improving church activities so that your church serves more people, and serves them better.

Quality and the Japanese Experience

Following World War II, much of Japan was in a shambles. Japanese exports were considered cheap junk or imitations.

In 1950, Dr. W. Edwards Deming, then a 49-year-old American statistician and engineer, was invited to Japan to present a series of lectures to Japanese business leaders. His ideas captured their imaginations, and they began to dream big dreams. With Dr. Deming's counsel, they designed new systems to produce quality goods. Those systems are capable of continued improvement, and they provide increasingly better products with fewer defects. Along with their new systems, the Japanese developed a new standard of quality for their products and services, and they garnered new respect (and envy) in world markets.

Dr. Deming and others offered that same formula for quality improvement to business leaders in the United States, but there were few takers. In the 1950s, United States industry led the world in quantity and quality of goods and saw no need for change. In less than a generation, however, the Japanese overtook the United States in the quality and sales of automobiles, high-tech equipment, and consumer goods.

The Deming formula for quality is known today by such names as TQM (Total Quality Management), QI (Quality Improvement), TQI (Total Quality Improvement), or TQL (Total Quality Leadership).

Dr. Deming's formula is based upon a surprisingly limited number of simple recommendations, all of which may be applied to the church . . .

- ◆ Listen to your customers for their definition of quality.
- ◆ Be clear about your aim — the results you want — and hold that aim inviolate.
- ◆ Learn to think systemically to understand how parts work together to provide a productive and smoothly functioning system.
- ◆ Learn to see work as process, rather than as problem solving.
- ◆ Design systems that are capable of and demand continual improvement.
- ◆ Provide leaders who take responsibility for managing systems to produce the desired aims.
- ◆ Remember that systems are designed for the results they get. If you want different or better results, you have to redesign your system.
- ◆ Remove barriers that prevent people from taking responsibility for the organization.
- ◆ Learn to measure variation in your system. A system that cannot consistently produce the same level of quality is unstable and cannot be managed adequately.
- ◆ Concentrate improvement efforts on the core process that will enable you to align the system toward the desired aim and will provide leverage for moving the organization in a different direction.

Some people have reservations about applying principles used in business and industry to service and nonprofit organizations. However, quality improvement processes have successfully been used to transform government, health, and educational institutions. In addition, the evidence supports the value of quality improvement processes in improving the ministry and service of churches and religious institutions.

Two Kinds of Knowledge

To achieve quality, we need to bring two kinds of knowledge together: (1) a basic understanding about the distinctive purposes and methods of church life and (2) knowledge for improvement.

We need knowledge of the church — knowledge of our history and traditions as a church; knowledge about worship, the Scriptures, the sacraments, prayer, and how the church has listened to and experienced God at work in creating and redeeming the world. In recent times, we have believed that this kind of knowledge — professional knowledge — was sufficient to operate and improve our churches.

However, we also need knowledge for improvement — knowledge of systems, the specific needs and searchings of the people in our communities, psychology and motivation, frameworks and theories for learning, theories of change, and how to achieve consistency in quality of service.

As church leaders, we begin with knowledge of the church and of the Christian tradition. Knowledge for improvement brings learnings from other disciplines to help us organize and manage the church so people can participate and so that we can continually improve the church for better outreach and service.

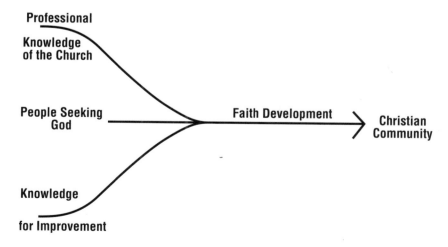

Quest for Quality is not a magic cure-all. It's not a method for controlling organizations and people. It's not a simple formula that produces quick results.

> Quest for Quality is not a magic cure-all. It's not a simple formula that produces quick results.

Quest is a distinctive view of the work of the church, people, and how the two intersect. It is a philosophy that is built upon and encourages the values of:

- Cooperation rather than competition.
- Listening to people rather than deciding for people.
- Using what we know and seeking deeper and broader knowledge.
- Trusting people and involving people in leading the processes in which they participate.
- Focusing on people and on their lives together in social systems rather than focusing only on products and results.
- Paying attention to the distinctive nature of the church and its ministry.
- Involving ourselves as co-creators with God to improve and extend what we have.

In the chapters that follow, we will introduce the philosophy and principles of "Quest for Quality." Throughout this book will be references to the "indispensable three" of Quest for Quality:

1. Clarify the aim.

2. Design a system to reach the aim.

3. Institute leadership to manage the system to reach that aim.

Quality improvement sounds simple, but it is not. It is hard work, and it may take a decade for many church organizations to turn around. But the task can be done. The journey is exciting as improvements begin and grow daily!

> *Quality improvement in the church is our human effort to be faithful to what God is doing in the world and in us. It is striving to respond with our best. It is sharing God's wonderful acts with others. It is seeking to be more caring and loving and to create more just relationships among people.*

CHAPTER 2

Getting Beyond the Expected

Quality is getting more than you expect. Quality is providing a service or product that is consistently superior. Every time the customer receives the service, it is the same, but better. Quality is a service or product that is produced by a system that is capable of producing an even better service or product tomorrow. As former President Jimmy Carter once said about something, "It is so good; it's too bad it's not better."

Quality, then, is not merely what meets the expectations of customers. Quality goes beyond expectations to delight and surprise people.

Quality is not a concept that can be defined universally. We can point to it. We know it when we see it. We can describe it or point to its characteristics. We can establish indicators for it. But we can define quality only in relation to the needs of people who use a product or service, their expectations, and the "over and above" possibility for the product or service.

On the one hand, we are saying that the people who receive and use a service or product are the ones who can judge it to be "quality." On the other hand, we are saying that people cannot define quality in advance because, by definition, quality is something better than people expect.

In the final analysis, quality *must be defined* by the people who *provide* the product or service. But the providers can define quality only by listening carefully to the customers or beneficiaries.

The people asked for better candles. The quality organization heard a desire for better light. It offered the incandescent lightbulb.

The students asked for a better slide rule. The quality organization heard their desire for ease and speed in mathematical computation and offered the personal calculator.

The people asked for better vacuum tubes in their radios and televisions. The quality organization heard their desire for better reliability and offered the transistor and the integrated circuit.

Quality can be defined *only by the producer* in the context of careful, patient, and persistent listening to the customers or beneficiaries.

Three Levels of Quality

Paul Batalden and the Quality Resource Group of HCA (Hospital Corporation of America) talk about three levels of quality: (1) Assumed, (2) Expected, and (3) Delighted.

LEVEL 1
"Assumed"; "Must have"; "Take it for granted."

When present, the intended beneficiaries are satisfied, but they may not notice that they are satisfied. If the assumed level of quality is missing, customers are not satisfied and may have strong negative reactions.

LEVEL 2
"Expected"; "Requested"; "Satisfied"; "Meets requirements."

Level 2 is the level of expectation. When present, there is no particular response, because past experience has conditioned people to expect this level. When more is given, people are more satisfied; when less is given, people are less satisfied.

LEVEL 3
"Delighted"; "Excited"; "So good it attracts me to it."

When this level of quality is absent, chances are no one will notice. But when it is present, people are pleased and surprised. It is this level of service that produces loyal customers.

Loyalty to brands, organizations (including church denominations), or services is not as prevalent as in the past. Only the "finest quality" holds loyalty. Level 2 quality will not do it, because others will provide Level 3 quality.

Let's look at some examples.

Air Travel

Assumed (Level 1)
> "The airplane will be able to take off, fly to my destination, and land safely."

Expected (Level 2)
> "The plane will arrive on time, and I will have my luggage when I leave the airport."

Delighted (Level 3)
> "The meal served was delicious. The flight attendants baked cookies for us right there on the plane — for all of us, those in economy class too!"

Hospital

Assumed (Level 1)
> "I expect to get the correct blood for my blood transfusion."

Expected (Level 2)
> "I went to have my hernia repaired. I expected it to hurt some, to be out the same day, and to receive a correct bill."

Delighted (Level 3)
> "Everyone treated me with respect, explained things carefully to me, and even called me at home the next day to see how I was doing."

Church

Assumed (Level 1)

> "I assume the church will have a choir and a nursery for my children, and that the pastor will preach a sermon."

Expected (Level 2)

> "I expect that the choir will sing on key and have music I know and like; the nursery will be clean, and my child will be happy when I return; and the sermon will be biblical and interesting."

Delighted (Level 3)

> "I found myself swept up by the beauty of the music and the sacred dance. The nursery teacher reported what the children had done during the hour and called on Monday to tell me of a special program for the next week. The sermon was easy to follow because of the outline printed in the bulletin. The service made me feel close to God and more concerned about other people."

Is this discussion about quality and improvement not also related to people's growth in grace, obedience, and faithful living? The faith of the Christian church is that God created us and all the world and continues to create and re-create. It is our faith, too, that God redeems our unworthy efforts and our very selves. We believe that through unmerited grace, God leads us to higher levels of faithfulness.

Quality improvement in the church is our human effort to be faithful to what God is doing in the world and in us. It is striving to respond with our best. It is sharing God's wonderful acts with others. It is seeking to be more caring and loving and to create more just relationships among people. It is creating the best possible context for people to be received into the Christian community, related to God, nurtured, and sent out to serve. Quality improvement is the disciples' attempt to be faithful in building vital congregations.

> Quality improvement in the church is our human effort to be faithful to what God is doing in the world and in us.

Quality in the church, as in any institution, is achieved in three ways:

1. Offering a service that delights the people we serve.
2. Reducing variation in the level of quality of the service so that quality becomes the expected level.
3. Building a system capable of improvement. If people expect to be delighted, an organization can maintain the third level of quality only by having a system in place that is capable of improvement and that produces a continually improving service.

All three ways of achieving quality must be pursued by a quality organization at the same time. If this happens, it will offer quality now, quality tomorrow, and quality in the future. When quality happens in the church, the loyalty and desire of the people to participate and to give themselves to the church's ministry is never in question.

> When quality happens in the church, the loyalty and desire of the people to participate and to give themselves to the church's ministry is never in question.

It would seem that quality is incremental — that it is "the expected," except better. That is true — but there is more.

Quality improvement theory holds that to consistently rise above the expected to quality services and quality systems that produce those services, a different way of thinking (different, that is, from the norms of our society today) is necessary. The whole organization has to have a different kind of vision driving it, a different system relating all the parts of the organization in an optimal way, and leaders who take a radically different approach to people and to processes. An organization may achieve occasional quality without such organizational transformation, but not consistent and continually improving quality.

Quest for Quality refers to a philosophy of leadership and understanding that is counter to management theories popular in our society in the past and current, for the most part, even today.

Quest for Quality	Current Norms
(Managers tell people what their jobs are)	*(Managers tell people how to do their jobs)*
Relies on self-motivation	Rely on external motivation
Focuses on the system	Focus is on goals
Is built on cooperation	Are built on competition
Sees work as process	See work as events, problems, or programs
Uses professional and improvement knowledge	Rely only on professional knowledge
Sees teamwork as essential	Require individuals to do their jobs
Improves systems	Set numerical goals
Relies on good data	Rely on hunches
Values knowledge	Value experience
Views long-term perspective	Set short-term goals
Reduces variation	If it's broken, fix it
Improves systems	Find people to blame
Employs horizontal flow	Employ top-down flow
Works on the whole	Work on the parts
Works on the core process	Do something, even if it's wrong
Involves long-term commitment	Involve high mobility

Two attributes of Quest for Quality are fundamental. The first is continuous improvement. In this understanding of quality, there is never a level at which the quality is good enough that it does not need to be improved. Whether moving from poor quality to better quality, or from fine quality to superior quality, the mandate of the quality philosophy is, "Find a way to improve it."

Reduce variation, redesign it, work on processes within it, deliver and market it better, offer better support services, or build better relations with customers. However it may be done, the first commandment of quality leadership is, "Continually and forever improve."

> The first commandment of quality leadership is, "Continually and forever improve."

The second distinctive characteristic of Quest for Quality is the emphasis on listening to the customers. The word *customer* is not a term normally used in relation to nonprofit institutions such as schools, hospitals, or government or religious organizations. Many people prefer terms such as *people*, *constituents*, *members*, *clients*, *beneficiaries*, or the like.

An even better term may be *stakeholder*. As used in quality improvement theory, *customer* refers to all the people who have a stake in the organization. Customers or stakeholders are the people who depend on the organization, feel ownership in it, spend a great deal of time in it, receive value from it, or are otherwise related to it.

Some teachers of quality improvement theory suggest that there are five categories of customers:

1. The people who receive the services or products of the organization
2. The workers who produce the products or services
3. Suppliers
4. The owners of the organization (in some cases, shareholders)
5. The community

In some institutions, each of the five groups of customers is distinct. In an automobile dealership, the car buyer, salesperson, owner, supplier, and community are different people. In a church or a school, on the other hand, one person may fill several roles concurrently. Typically, a person fits one or two categories at a particular time and may fill another role at another time.

The distinction of quality improvement is that the customers are heard. Elitist thinking or actions are usually the result of failing to listen to the

customers. Visionary leaders hear their people. Listening to customers —
all five groups of them — is vital.

The leader of a quality organization has the task of getting each process
in the system working at its best relational level with all the processes of
the system. Having parts working at *appropriate* levels in the system is more
important than having each part working at its highest or best level.

A person does not have a quality lifestyle when he or she has unlimited
food for breakfast and no food at lunch or dinner. It is not quality for one's
heart to beat faster than the rest of the body can tolerate, or for salespeople
to sell more products than manufacturing can produce. To "sub-optimize"
is to concentrate improvement of quality in one part of an organization,
even though it can't fully contribute to a higher level of quality in the
whole organization because other processes are functioning at lower levels.

> To "sub-optimize" is to concentrate improvement of quality
> in one part of an organization, even though it can't fully
> contribute to a higher level of quality in the whole
> organization because other processes are functioning at
> lower levels.

Sub-optimization takes place when leaders fail to listen to *all* their
customers. It happens when some customers are served at the expense of
others.

Those who receive the service or product want good value or results for
money or energy expended. Workers want good pay in exchange for their
labor. If the end beneficiaries receive something beyond optimal value (at
a price much too low, for example), the workers may have to take reduced
pay for their services if the organization is to continue. For example, an
airline locked in a struggle with its competitors might lower its ticket prices
below profitability, causing flight attendants and other employees to have
to forego salary increases. Failure to secure paper, ink, and manuscripts at a
reasonable rate may cause a publishing company to go out of business,
resulting in losses for employees and shareholders alike.

Problems with a church's financial giving system may mean fewer services for outreach to the community. Pastors who spend inordinate amounts of time in individual counseling sessions may not have adequate time for listening to and serving others in the parish. An excellent music program in worship may reveal the lack of quality in other parts of the worship service — or vice versa. Similarly, adding new facilities without adding adequate parking is counterproductive.

Quality is quality only when it is total quality — quality for all the customers. Quality is possible only when all the customers are heard.

Quality results when all customers are heard and all processes and systems are designed and continually improved so that higher levels of quality are achieved.

Finally, quality is caring. It is caring about people. Quality is listening to people and responding to them. Quality is caring enough about all the people related to an organization to make them feel special, to give them the best, and to improve continually.

> *In the context of the church's mission of faith development, leaders can articulate a vision for the church's ministry, a comprehensive picture of what the church's ministry might be in the future. This vision draws them forward into the future. It comes out of the deepest yearnings of the people and a realistic understanding of the world the church serves. The shared vision comes out of dialogue between the leaders and the people, is stated and described by the leader, and is supported by all the people.*

CHAPTER 3

Mission and Vision

The quality church has a clearly defined mission, and it aligns all its activities toward achieving that mission.

Every organization has a mission. The simplest way to think about the mission is to answer the question, "What business are we in?" For example, a worker in a school might say he or she is in the business of educating or socializing the young. A hospital worker might reply that he or she is in the business of health care.

People who work in or manage the affairs of a church or church-related institution might say they are in the business of faith development. Others might call it spiritual formation or spiritual growth, but however they say it, the mission is to assist people in their yearning to live in harmony with God and with one another.

In the context of the church's mission of faith development, leaders can articulate a vision for the church's ministry, a comprehensive picture of what the church's ministry might be in the future. This vision draws them forward into the future. It comes out of the deepest yearnings of the people and a realistic understanding of the world the church serves. The shared vision comes out of dialogue between the leaders and the people, is stated and described by the leader, and is supported by all the people.

The church's vision, coming out of the hearts of the people, extends the personal vision of all who participate. It embraces what people want from God and how they want to praise God and celebrate God's good gifts. It includes their longings and hopes for themselves, their family and friends, and their communities.

> The church's vision, coming out of the hearts of the people, extends the personal vision of all who participate.

Some congregations write mission statements or vision statements. For many, the mission statement should be simple — a short phrase. Vision statements, if they are too wordy, may be counterproductive. Visions are images in our minds. They can be talked about and sometimes expressed in pictures or artistic forms, but it is more difficult to describe them adequately in prose. The important thing is to clarify the mission and to image and state the vision clearly and concisely.

When Jesus called the disciples, their mission was to follow Jesus.
Their vision was to be fishers of people.

Paul's mission in his later life was to give guidance to the faith communities that had been organized in places throughout the Roman Empire.
His vision was people who imaged the values of Christ rather than the values of the Jewish leaders or of secular society.

St. Augustine's mission was to lead the church.
His vision was the church as the "City of God."

Martin Luther King Jr.'s mission was integration and civil rights.
His vision was all people living together in love.

John Wesley's mission was renewal of the church.
His vision was "to spread scriptural holiness."

Our mission is the renewal of the church.
Our vision is every United Methodist congregation vital, alive, and fulfilling its
   primary task in its community.

A congregation or church organization that has a clear vision or aim
can assess its present position in relation to the vision. The gap between
present reality and the vision is the area for improvement. A system can
be built that will help the organization close the gap.

You can't design a system if you don't know where you are going.
You need to be clear about mission and vision.

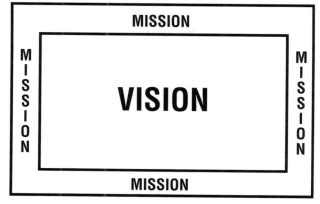

Think of it this way. The mission is a picture frame for the artist. The
artist is the leader of the church. The picture frame provides the boundary
for the vision of the congregation. The mission— the frame — defines the
nature of the organization, the setting for the church's activity.

The vision is the picture in the frame. It is always set in the context of
the mission. The vision originates in the minds and hearts of the people.
It is formed as a whole in the mind and imagination of the leader. It is then
painted and communicated back to the people. The people recognize it,
identify with it, and commit to it — because it is theirs.

> The vision is the picture in the frame. It is always set in the
> context of the mission.

Quest for Quality is about clarifying the vision or aim. It is also about building a system to move from where we are to where we want to go. That is the task of leadership and all who belong to or participate in the church.

Not just any system will do. The system must deliver the vision that is imaged in the minds and hearts of the people, articulated by the leader, and pursued and supported by all.

In his video *The Power of Vision*, Joel Barker elaborates on the relationship between vision and a system for reaching it. He says the vision, once imaged and stated, draws the organization to it and provides the blueprint for the journey.

Think about family members who plant a garden. Their vision must fit with their mission. If their mission is providing food, their vision might be a luscious green garden, well fertilized, with ample rain and no pests.

If their mission is a family project to provide togetherness, their vision may be of evenings with all members of the family going about their designated tasks for the good of the whole. The vision here will not omit the hoped-for ample produce, but the vision is centered on the processes of working together and being together rather than on the fruits of their labors.

The most important first step in any organization or any endeavor is clarity of aim — of mission and vision. Without such clarity, you can't build a system. Without a system and leaders to make it work, an organization — yes, even a church — will founder and die.

> *After clarifying our vision — in our search for quality in the church — our next step is to design a system that will allow our vision to become reality. A system is an interdependent group of people, processes, functions, and activities that work together for a common aim.*

CHAPTER 4
Systems and Processes

If you don't know where you want to go, you can't design a means to get there. If you do know where you want to go, and you expect to get there, you must have a method appropriate to the task.

If I am in Nashville and want to go to Memphis, Tennessee, I have several choices of transportation — auto, bus, plane, bicycle, or walking. If I want to go to Memphis, Egypt, I may choose to travel by ship or by plane. The system that will get me to Memphis, Tennessee, will look very different from the system that will get me to Memphis, Egypt.

A system will deliver the results it is designed for — no more and not something different. A system designed to get me to Memphis, Tennessee, will not get me to Memphis, Egypt.

After clarifying our vision — in our search for quality in the church — our next step is to design a system that will allow our vision to become reality. A system is an interdependent group of people, processes, functions, and activities that work together for a common aim.

There are several parts or processes in a system. In most systems, there are hundreds and thousands of parts, but there must be at least two parts.

In a system, *the parts must work together.* They are interdependent rather than independent. Each part or process is important. Each one fills a role, but each one also interacts with other parts. The parts of a system must have a common aim, and their work together must be for the purpose of attaining that aim.

A ball team is usually a system. The players work together to win. If the "team" is really an informal collection of individuals, playing for fun, with no strategy and no particular objective in mind, it may not be a system. In professional sports, a football, baseball, or basketball team must operate as a system. A bowling team usually is not a system. There is a common aim of winning, but each player operates independently.

Other examples of systems are an orchestra, the human body, an automobile, or a business.

Most systems are subsystems of a larger system. Many systems have subsystems within their make-up.

The United Methodist Church is a system. An annual conference is a subsystem of The United Methodist Church and a system in its own right. A congregation is also a system, even as it is a subsystem of the conference and a sub-subsystem of The United Methodist Church.

> ## The United Methodist Church is a system.

Let's focus on The United Methodist Church. The whole is formed by many parts, processes, and interworkings fitting appropriately together. The United Methodist system includes local churches, missions, schools, colleges, community centers, homes, hospitals, districts, annual conferences, circuits and larger parishes, bishops and district superintendents, General Conference, general and conference agencies, seminaries, and publishing houses.

Our system embraces all we are, all we do, and how we do it. The task of our Quest for Quality in The United Methodist Church is to strengthen and improve the system. It is to check on the parts; to look at fit and relationships; and to review the aim — the mission and vision — toward which everything points. The task, then, depending on the type of intervention and leadership called for, is to rebuild the system or to improve it.

The building blocks of systems are processes. A process is a sequential grouping of all the tasks directed at accomplishing an outcome. It is "inputs" being transformed into "outputs." A process has three parts — input, transformation, and output — just like a computer.

System

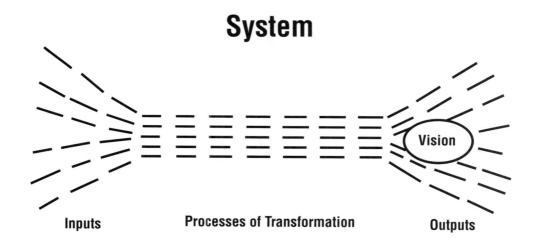

Inputs   **Processes of Transformation**   **Outputs**

The process may be quite simple. We can all identify with the following examples:

Input	Transformation	Output
Soiled laundry	Washing machine	Clean laundry
New pencil	Pencil sharpener	Pencil with fine point
Seed	Seed sprouts and grows	Flowers or vegetables
People	Church	Disciples

Some processes have multiple inputs, transformation cycles, or outputs:

Input	Transformation	Output
Film	Developing	Pictures
Other Materials		Slides

Input	Transformation	Output
Air	Breathing	Healthy person
Food	Digestion	
	Circulation	

Work may be understood as solving problems, doing things, holding events, or maintaining and improving processes. Thinking of our work (at the factory, office, or church) as process allows us to view the whole of the transaction, to relate outcomes to all that has produced them, and then to place the whole process in the context of other related processes. When viewed this way, the actor is better able to understand how an intervention in the system will affect the whole system and its results. Failure to take a systems or process perspective may lead to solutions to problems that cause even greater problems, inefficiencies, or poor results.

> Failure to take a systems or process perspective may lead to solutions to problems that cause even greater problems, inefficiencies, or poor results.

Just as systems may break down when one or more parts do not work well, or work well together, or work toward a common aim, processes may also need to be repaired or improved. Actually, we improve systems by improving processes. Sometimes we need to improve, add to, or change the inputs. At other times, we need to alter the transformation phase.

At other times, we may seek to change the outputs for the good of the whole system by working on both the inputs and the transformation phase. Systems that work well to produce intended results have processes and subsystems aligned together, working for the good of the whole. Each process has a unique role. Not all parts do the same things, but in an optimal system, there are neither too many parts or processes nor too few. One small part — such as a battery — may keep a whole automobile from working. Having two batteries when only one is needed is costly, adds to the overhead of the system, and reduces its "value."

In brief, the process of Quest for Quality is:

1. *Clarify the aim* of the system.

2. *Evaluate* to determine whether to improve the present system or build a new system.

3. *Identify key processes* within the system — or key subsystems — which, if improved, will provide leverage for total system improvement.

4. *Form teams* of people who have responsibility for constellations of processes to study those processes and act to improve them.

5. *Provide team members with the knowledge, skills, and disciplines* they need to improve the processes of their parts of the system.

6. *The leader then makes sure that all processes and subsystems are aligned* together to achieve the purposes for which the system was established.

Systems are complex and are often beyond the scope of one person's understanding. Most of the members of an organizational system do not and cannot grasp or even think about the whole system, nor should they! Each person needs different things from the organization and has different contributions to offer.

But one person, the leader, must know about, understand, and take responsibility for the entire system. That is the difference between the leader and the rest of the people related to a church or any organization.

Our discussion here has reminded us again of the indispensable three of Quest for Quality:

1. Clarity of mission and vision.

2. A system designed and functioning to deliver the vision that is identified, shared, and pursued by the people.

3. Leaders who understand and have the knowledge and skills to keep the system on track, repair it, improve it, and finally change it as visions and circumstances change.

The system is designed for the results it is getting. If you want different results, you have to change or improve the system.

Perhaps it is worth saying again: "The system is designed for the results it is getting. If you want different results, you have to change or improve the system."

> *The **primary task** is what an organization must do in a particular environment at a particular time to carry out its basic mission and survive.*
>
> *If the **primary task** is not working in an organization, the organization is essentially dead. The **primary task** is the core of activities that produces the core product or service of the institution.*

CHAPTER 5
The Primary Task/Core Process

We have learned that processes are three-part transactions — whether simple or complex — that relate with other processes to form systems. Systems are the methods or means for organizations to achieve their aims.

A process changes inputs into outputs. It takes parts of a system and relates them together to produce one or more new "parts" that are needed for the system to work well. Good inputs acted upon by a well-planned transformation cycle will give good outputs.

Most systems have many processes working individually and together. Each process was planned for a purpose and designed to do a specific job. Many processes that work well day in and day out go unnoticed. They go unnoticed because they work well. As one or more processes break down, we may notice a "problem." We act to fix the recalcitrant process or processes, and the system works again.

Incidentally, the usual pattern is to repair processes only when they are broken and demand fixing. One of the primary tenets of the Quest for Quality is that to get quality — and keep quality — you have to work to improve the processes of the system continually, even when they seem to be working acceptably.

Underlying the many individual processes that function together in a system to produce the intended aim is a **core process** or **primary task**. The core process, like the other processes in the system, has input, a transformation cycle, and output. However, it is unique. There can be only one **core process** in a system. If you can find more than one, you either have more than one system operating, or you haven't yet identified **the core process**.

In the church we use the terms *primary task* and *core process* inter-changeably. (Jim Anderson and I borrowed the term *primary task* from A. K. Rice for our book *The Management of Ministry*, first published in 1978.) The primary task of a system is the system's most basic transaction. It is built upon the organization's mission and gives life and specificity to that mission.

The primary task is what an organization must do in a particular environment at a particular time to carry out its basic mission and survive. The primary task comprises the essential processes related in a system that must be present to fulfill customers' minimal expectations. It is the basic work of the organization.

If the primary task is not working in an organization, the organization is essentially dead. The primary task is the core of activities that produces the core product or service of the institution. It is the lifeblood, the heart and soul, the bread and butter.

The primary task is the most basic task in the system. The primary input in the system is called the "throughput." Identifying the core "throughput" or primary entity that moves through a system, and then identifying the major stages through which it goes, is often the most helpful way to clarify the primary task.

The core process is the one central series of input → change → output activities that provides the greatest leverage for rebuilding or improving an organization that is in disrepair. By the same token, when building a new organization, the designer should begin with the core process.

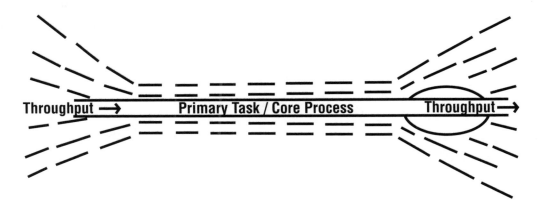

Throughput → **Primary Task / Core Process** Throughput →

Another way to think about the core process is to envision the fundamental steps in a system that can bring all the other processes in the system into alignment. The alignment of processes is not possible without a core. Identify it, and you have found the core process.

Clarifying an organization's mission and identifying its core process may be difficult. Generally, if you can solve one of those mysteries, you can solve the other, because the core process clarifies the major stages of the mission.

Let's try some examples:

1. The mission of a fine restaurant is to provide a memorable dining experience for the people who live, visit, or travel in the community. The core throughput is people. The core process is:

Seeking →	*Greeting →*	*Receiving →*	*Serving →*	*Receiving*
customers	*and hosting*	*the order and*	*the food to*	*payment*
	customers	*preparing food*	*customers*	
		for customers		

2. The mission of the water department of the county government is to provide good, safe, potable water. The core throughput is water. The core process is:

Taking water →	*Filtering and →*	*Piping it to →*	*Reading →*	*Billing and*
from the river	*purifying it*	*the customer*	*the meters*	*receiving payment*

3. The mission of a tailor shop is to provide clothing. The core throughput is cloth. The core process is:

Making or → Measuring the → Making the → Fitting the → Receiving
buying the   customer   clothes   clothes   payment
cloth

4. The mission of the office of the attorney general is to clarify state laws. The core throughput is a legal question. The core process is:

Receiving → Researching → Analyzing → Writing → Delivering
legitimate   the questions   the data   opinions   opinions
questions

5. The mission of a hospital is delivering health care. The core throughput is people. The core process is:

Admit → Gather → Determine → Implement → Evaluate → Release
patients   information   treatment   treatment   treatment   patients
*   plan   plan   plan*

6. The mission of a college is building knowledge for living. The core throughput is people. The core process is:

Recruiting → Admitting → Planning → Registering → Teaching → Assessing
students   students   for learning   students for   and   learning
*   courses   learning*

After assessment, there is the additional step of assisting with the transition to the workplace.

The core process is often difficult to define. One reason is that there may be so many major processes at work in the organization, all of which are important, that it is hard to focus on one or to get beneath all of them to define the primary throughput and primary process.

Service organizations are different from manufacturing or product-related organizations in their definitions of core process. The core throughput in manufacturing is generally a product. In service organizations, the core throughput is generally people — the customers.

> Service organizations are different from manufacturing or product-related organizations in their definitions of core process.

Another difficulty in defining the core process is getting clarity about the core beneficiaries or customers. Generally there is more than one major beneficiary or customer to be pleased. As we discussed in chapter 2, it is helpful to think of five groups of customers: (1) the people receiving the service or product; (2) the owners or stockholders; (3) the employees, including volunteer workers; (4) the suppliers; (5) the community and the environment.

Often, maximizing benefits for one of these groups means offering less to another. Balancing and optimizing benefits for all these groups is necessary — but difficult. How leaders deal with this issue will determine how they define core throughput and core process. For example, in a teaching hospital, is the core throughput the student doctors and nurses or the patients? In a graduate school of a university, is the mission teaching and learning or research? The answer will affect the definition of the core process.

All these difficulties come into play as we define the mission, core throughput, and core process of churches and religious institutions.

Let's begin with your congregation. What is the mission?

Faith development?   *Preaching the Word?*
Making disciples?   *Offering the sacraments?*
Church growth?   *Building a strong institution?*
Christian service?   *Christian community?*
Place of retreat and meditation?

There must be at least a hundred ways to state the mission. However, it is important that you clarify the mission of your congregation because everything you do — including how you envision results and build or improve a system to reach those results — depends on the mission.

The core throughput in the congregational system is also defined by how you state the mission. In the examples just given, the core throughputs could be people, the Scriptures, congregations or subgroups within it, programs, rituals, or statistics. The core process will vary according to the core throughput.

In the General Board of Discipleship, we have wrestled with questions of mission and core process for a dozen years, and we continue to do so. We continually try to improve how we talk about these concepts. Our present statement of mission for the congregation is simply "faith development" because we believe the fundamental task of the church is helping people develop their faith.

The core throughput of the congregation, we believe, is people. The core process is:

- *Reaching out and receiving people into the congregation.*
- *Helping them strengthen their relationship to God through Christ.*
- *Nurturing them in the Christian faith and equipping them for lives of discipleship.*
- *Sending them out to live as God's people — extending the church and helping make the world more loving and just.*

THE CONGREGATION

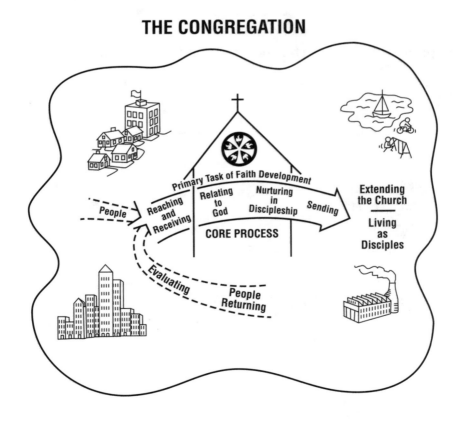

Others use different words and sometimes different concepts to state the central task of the church. The long-range strategy committee of one church defines its core process as:

1. Meeting and greeting other questing persons.

2. Inviting persons to a new way of living.

3. Relating people to God.

4. Relating people to one another — building community.

5. Responding to being forgiven.

One way of stating the task is not superior to the other. What is important is that you state it for your church and that you design a system with those processes at its core so that the results you get are the results you want. Briefly let us review what we have learned:

1. A quality organization producing quality services or products works intentionally and continually to clarify its aim — its mission and vision. It then builds a system and manages it to produce the desired aim.

2. Building a system aligned with an organization's mission or aim is begun by identifying the primary task. The primary task gives reality to the mission and provides the central core around which other major tasks and support tasks may be aligned.

3. Stating the core process is made easier by identifying the core throughput of the system. Stating the core process is also facilitated by asking which series of activities will give the most leverage in reaching the organizational aim if the series is rebuilt or improved. Where can we get the quickest payoff and the most lasting improvement? What do we most need to do to get on track or stay on track?

It is challenging and difficult to reconceptualize the work of the church and to design a system that will enable the people of the church to carry out that work with continuing improvement. Even more challenging is determining where to begin to change the system. It is the role of the core process to help us over this hurdle.

The core process helps us clarify what is essential in the organization. It helps us distinguish between what we *must* do and what we *can* do.

This task, which is primary and basic, gives us the core around which a whole new system can be designed and built. When it is improved, the whole organization improves.

Simplifying a complex system in order to work on it is the first step for most of us. The core process lets us do that. It then becomes the centerpiece for working on all the other major processes.

Finally, action to improve the core process in most organizations will produce significant, immediate change. When the pressure is for short-term results — as is true of most of Western society — this early improvement encourages and sustains us for the long-term journey of continuing improvement.

As the decades have gone by and values supporting individualism have grown and matured, the nature and culture of The United Methodist Church have changed. We have spoken a connectional, covenantal polity, while the reality of our life and work has become congregational and individualistic.

> *We "lost our watch" in the gradual change from connectionalism to congregationalism, and we are searching for it in each of our 35,000 congregations.*

CHAPTER 6

The Lost Watch and the Annual Conference

The story is told of a drunken man who lost his watch and was searching for it at night under a lamppost. When a passerby asked him where he had lost the watch, the man replied that it was some distance away, but in a dark place. He explained that he had chosen to look for the watch where there was light.

The man in the story may not be as inept as we might think. He knew that he needed two things to find his watch: He needed to look where he lost it, and he needed light. Since he didn't have both, he chose one. Most of us would have chosen another alternative, such as waiting for daylight or getting a portable light source. In his inebriated state, he probably could not think beyond two simple options.

Let us turn now to the story of The United Methodist Church.

The Methodist Church is more than 200 years old. Before it was even a hundred years old, it began to lose its role as the largest American Protestant Church — a standing it had accomplished in record time in its early days as it moved westward across the nation. The failure to extend the church's ministry at or better than the pace of population growth began in the late nineteenth century, but the consistent decline in size from previous levels of membership and participation did not begin until the last third of the twentieth century. Just as the man who lost his watch was not able to connect the place for looking with the light for looking, United Methodists have generally not been able to connect the loss of extent of ministry a hundred years ago with the loss in actual membership in recent years. We have sought contemporary reasons for the decline:

- ◆ We are no longer a Christian nation.
- ◆ The church has more competition.
- ◆ People are more secular.
- ◆ We quit doing things the "old-time" way.

However, the real reason for the decline may be traced to changes that began more than a century ago.

But there is more. We may not only be looking for the root causes of decline in the wrong century, but also at the wrong place — the wrong part of the United Methodist system. The United Methodist Church is a connectional system that depends on several levels of church life to operate effectively. The basic system of The United Methodist Church is the annual conference. It says so in the constitution of the church, and it was clearly the reality in John Wesley's lifetime.

This connectional church, when transported to the extreme individualistic culture of America, was transplanted in alien soil. As the decades have gone by and values supporting individualism have grown and matured, the nature and culture of The United Methodist Church have changed. We have spoken a connectional, covenantal polity, while the reality of our life and work has become congregational and individualistic.

We did not notice that the denomination was in serious disarray until both our laity and clergy no longer spoke the language of the connection. When they began, each in different ways, to lobby for individual rights for the clergy and congregational autonomy for their churches, we began to acknowledge a problem. We have been acting as though we were experiencing problems that with adequate patience we would resolve. We "lost our watch" in the gradual change from connectionalism to congregationalism (primarily at the conference and general church levels), and we are searching for it in each of our 35,000 congregations. To say it another way, we lost the watch at the annual conference level of the church, and we are trying to find it at the local church level.

Accompanying the shift from connectionalism to congregationalism is the shift from covenanted collegial leadership — pastors recruited, trained, and supported to lead a common ministry in all the congregations — to volunteer candidates for leadership, untested, trained at their whims, nurtured any way they individually can find help, and evaluated not at all. It is a shift from the *called* to the *profession*; from "Together we will seek the best way for all of us" to "I will do it my way." Congregations are whipsawed, led in one direction; and with a change in pastors, led in another direction.

The change that has occurred in leadership is the most serious of all. With good leaders, we could alter our search. We could begin to look for our United Methodist "watch" in the right times and places. Without good leadership, we are destined to continue more of the same.

The responsibility for providing leadership for the congregations belongs to the annual conference. Candidates are drawn from the congregations, for the most part. Ideally, the conference tests those candidates for pastoral leadership abilities and evidence of a divine call, trains them, nurtures and provides credentials for them, deploys them in pastoral ministry, and evaluates their work and their continuing need for support and training.

This series of annual conference responsibilities is the *core process of the annual conference*. It is the process of leadership development for the church's mission of faith development.

The annual conference is the place in the United Methodist system that can provide leverage for system improvement and for aligning all the other processes that must work together to ensure the strength of the total church's ministry. The annual conference's core process is the one precondition that will enable congregations to understand and carry out their core process of faith development.

THE ANNUAL CONFERENCE

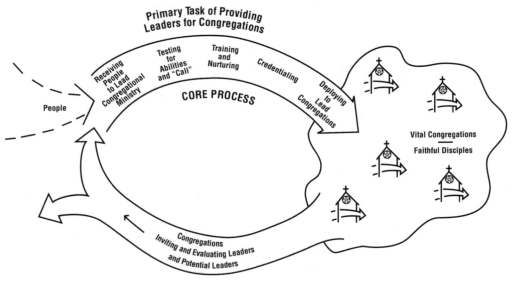

Primary Task of Providing Leaders for Congregations

Receiving People to Lead Congregational Ministry

Testing for Abilities and "Call"

Training and Nurturing

Credentialing

Deploying to Lead Congregations

CORE PROCESS

People

Vital Congregations
—
Faithful Disciples

Congregations Inviting and Evaluating Leaders and Potential Leaders

---

The annual conference's core process is the one precondition that will enable congregations to understand and carry out their core process of faith development.

The primary focus of the church's ministry is people.

The primary place of ministry is the congregation.

The primary relationship — which is the ministry of the church — is the relationship between the church and the people of the community it serves. It is the church reaching out into that community, receiving people, relating them to God, developing them as faithful disciples, and sending them out to live as changed and changing people, caring for their neighbors and building a better world.

The basic body in the church is the annual conference. It is the switchboard, the central control system, the catalyst that optimizes the ministry in the congregations and in their communities.

The primary place for maintaining the denomination's heritage and for remembering the lessons learned by the church since its days as a sect within the Jewish tradition is the General Conference. It is there that theological matters are worked on, direction is set, and parameters are identified for the whole church.

Local churches, annual conferences, and the General Conference compose a system. Each subsystem has an important role. When the system is working, we try to improve the major processes and keep the support processes in good working order. When the whole system is not working, the effects may show up in the strangest places. Sometimes they are near the lightpost; sometimes they are not. We don't want to make the mistake that the man in our opening story made — to make a choice and start looking. Rather, we want to examine the core process of the congregation, the annual conference, and the general church. We can then work to improve this core process at every level.

The annual conference is the place to begin our efforts. In our connectional system, it is the basic body of the church. Its primary task is the core process of the whole system. It also happens to be the place where we get leaders to initiate and facilitate the change in the whole system. It is at the annual conference level that we are most likely to find our watch — to find out what action will deliver the results we want. It is here that we can take action and begin the long trek forward to build a United Methodist system for the twenty-first century that will produce the finest quality we can imagine.

A leader has responsibility for all the relationships that mold all the parts into a working, task-accomplishing whole.

One of the unique characteristics of leadership is that "the problem" can never be outside the leader's responsibility.

*Quest for Quality begins with the leader.
You can get only the amount of quality in an
organization that the leader is capable of
and disposed to leading.*

CHAPTER 7

Leadership

I n any functioning organization or group, there are several jobs to be
done. But there is one job that is substantively different from all the
rest. It puts the person who does that job in a separate category. Whether
chosen by the group or placed in the position by outside decisions, this
person has a unique job. It may not be better, more important, or require
a higher I.Q., but it is different. The job is that of the leader.

Often, people ascribe the highest status and remuneration to the
leadership role, but its major attribute is that it is different in kind. A
person's ability to do other jobs does not automatically prepare him or
her for a leadership role. It is different.

Some of the knowledge needed for leadership is the same needed to do
many of the other jobs in an organization, but it also demands other kinds
of knowledge. Personality and personal values and the ability to relate to
people and to understand them are central to the leadership role, but the

primary distinction goes beyond these attributes.

Most workers have a set job to do and a particular sphere of control. They have a defined set of processes assigned to them. They need to understand those processes and how to relate them to a few other parts of the system. In short, a worker has responsibility for "a part" and its immediate relationship to a few other "parts." A leader has responsibility for *all the relationships* that mold *all the parts* into a working, task-accomplishing whole — and this is the all-important difference.

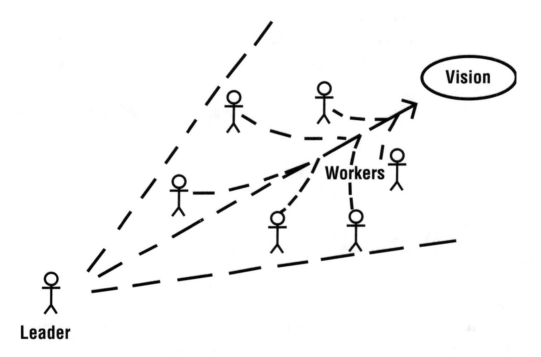

The leader in an organization that is committed to quality:

1. Defines the aim of the organization.
2. States the values of the organization.
3. Clarifies the boundaries of the organization in the context of its larger environment.
4. Articulates a vision for all members or workers.
5. Keeps the focus on the customers or beneficiaries.
6. Insists on continual improvement.

7. Points and relates improvement efforts to the primary task (the core process).
8. Sets standards for quality.
9. Takes primary responsibility for quality.
10. Recognizes the structure in work.
11. Sees work as process.
12. Steers the organization to reach its aim.
13. Maintains unity of purpose.
14. Looks for faults in operating systems, rather than blaming people.
15. Makes learning and training the hallmarks of the organization.
16. Removes barriers that prevent people from finding fulfillment in their work.

Again, the role of leader is fundamentally different from all other roles. Some people lead well; others do not. It appears that some people can learn to lead while others cannot. Sometimes a follower is put in a leadership role. As a good worker, who has always done his or her job, he or she defines the job and attempts to do it. However, this person then sees the leadership role as one more job. He or she then takes responsibility for one part and its limited relationship to other parts. The result is that the organization is leaderless.

Sometimes no one realizes that the leader is not leading until it is too late. He or she is doing the defined job well, so it is perceived that the problem is elsewhere. One of the unique characteristics of leadership is that "the problem" can never be outside the leader's responsibility. If there is a problem, or if the system is not working to attain the desired aim, it is the responsibility of the leader, even if his or her job has been defined differently. It is this characteristic that best shows the distinctiveness of the leadership role.

Quest for Quality begins with the leader. You can get only the amount of quality in an organization that the leader is capable of and disposed to leading.

When the leader is committed to quality, to improving the organization's system and output to the level of delighting the customers, quality improvement is possible. The leader has to manage the organization to improve the system and steer it to anticipated results. Without the leader's commitment and involvement, quality improvement cannot happen.

For many positions in an organization, relatively specific and clear job descriptions can be articulated — but not for the leader. The leadership role in any organization in its most generic form is to:

1. Clarify the aim.

2. Install a system that will deliver the aim.

3. Manage the system to deliver the aim.

Managing the system to deliver the aim is one of the most difficult tasks. What is done depends on . . .

- ◆ The context.
- ◆ How close the organization is to achieving its previously stated aim.
- ◆ The nature of the organization.
- ◆ Conditions in that sector (religion, government, business, etc.) at the time.
- ◆ The confluence of past history and present outlook.

Every day, many times a day, the leader must make decisions, the consequences of which are unknown. There is never adequate information, knowledge, or skills. Finances are always limited. Customers or beneficiaries of the organization have changing tastes and criteria for judging quality. Moreover, there are so many different groups to try to please.

> The leader must make decisions, the consequences of which are unknown.

Past mistakes haunt the leader. Past successes have not been adequately evaluated to ascertain why they were successes.

But judgments have to be made; and they are made. All the decisions in an organization flow from the decisions made by the leader.

Some helpful insights about leadership have been made by Dr. Paul Batalden, who leads the Quality Resource Group of Hospital Corporation of America. He observes:

1. Leaders are, first of all, *learners* and teachers. As such, they are models of quality improvement.

2. One of the jobs of management is *prediction*. We create the future through analysis and systems thinking.

3. Leaders are *drivers of change*.

4. Leaders see and understand the organization as a system and *manage the relationships* among the parts to integrate the system. Leaders are responsible for seeing that the organization is tied together. Often, people manage as though the parts of the organization were not connected.

5. Leaders are *experts at building knowledge for improvement* and integrating it with professional knowledge. Leaders create a learning environment and practice learning. People need to see improvement and to be encouraged as learners. Empowerment occurs when knowledge is imparted.

6. Leaders demonstrate their desire to continually improve their own management. One way is *seeking feedback* — "How am I doing?" "How are we doing?"

7. Leaders once spent a great amount of time exercising control. We now know that leaders need to spend greater and greater portions of time on *improvement*. We never get to the place where we can spend all the time on improvement.

8. Leaders especially need to understand *core process*, which helps them understand linkages in the organization and helps them direct their efforts and focus the improvement. Management keeps the focus on the core process.

9. Leaders understand intrinsic motivation. They evaluate the things they own — policies, habits, and traditions — to see if they can change those things that diminish intrinsic motivation. They identify toxic policies and habits.

Rebuilding and re-establishing The United Methodist Church as a vibrant institution with a vital ministry is a possibility. Ford Motor Company re-established itself in the world of automobiles. Harley Davidson reclaimed its quality image in the world of motorcycles. Nike did so in the world of sports shoes.

Rebuilding The United Methodist Church is a possibility worth pursuing. It will take leadership different from what some of us are exhibiting now.

> Rebuilding The United Methodist Church is a possibility worth pursuing.

With the task, come other realities:

(1) There are no blueprints. Rebuilding a mainline church has not been done in Protestantism before.

(2) The vision will not be a remade picture of the past. Where we are going is different from where we have been.

(3) Developing something out of nothing is creative and glamorous; rebuilding out of the used and broken is thankless and tedious.

(4) The United Methodist Church is incapable of renewal as a denomination. Renewal will happen, if it happens at all, one annual conference at a time. One annual conference finding new vitality through quality improvement will encourage others to be willing to try.

(5) Only one person in an annual conference can initiate and direct the change — the bishop. Others may call for it and point to needed changes, but change at the conference level is the bishop's responsibility. Pastors have the same responsibility in congregations. As they lead the change, others can join in.

(6) Disciplinary changes will be necessary for complete change to occur, but they are possible only after the renewal is well along. Early steps in the process will make other changes possible.

(7) It will take several quadrennia for annual conference and congregational renewal to be complete.

(8) Two types of knowledge are necessary for renewal — knowledge of the Christian church and knowledge of improvement in organizational systems. United Methodists seem to have the first, but not the second.

For people living now, the year 2000 and a new century may seem a long way off. However, for those who are ready to bring renewal to the church, there is barely enough time to upgrade the quality of our ministry for the new century.

The **first** critical question of leadership is whether the leader has the ability to listen to people and to state their shared vision.

The **second** critical question of leadership is whether the leader can hold the vision, while at the same time designing and constructing a system to give life to the vision.

The **third** critical question of leadership is determining how much change the leader can lead.

The **final** critical question is whether the leader is willing to change himself or herself.

> *The change in the leader becomes a declaration of the seriousness of the mission, the significance of the vision, and the kind of radical measures that are necessary to achieve it.*

CHAPTER 8

Why Should I Change?
A New Paradigm for Leadership

S ome people who occupy important leadership positions recently gathered to talk about their views of effective leadership. Their composite picture of a good leader follows:

> *I am the leader of this organization. I didn't put myself here. I was selected through normal processes. I must have some leadership qualities, or I would not have been chosen. I don't see any reason to change who I am, the way I work, or the way I relate to people.*
>
> *This organization was in serious trouble before I came to this position. I was chosen to get things moving again. Those who selected me for the position told me that I had the leadership qualities this organization needed.*

I have been here a while now, and we are beginning to see some changes. It takes a few years sometimes, particularly in a complex institution like this, to get to know people, to learn the "lay of the land," and to get structures established to move in new directions.

We have already done some good things here, and our people feel good about them. They like doing new things, trying new programs, and being creative. The traditions around here, when I came, were stifling. Nothing had been changed for decades. No wonder the organization was not doing well. The staff needed a leader who was willing to try something new. I have done that, and the spirit here is already better.

People can change only so much, however. I am already changing things faster than some people want. But we are moving. We just have to have patience.

Why do I believe that what we are doing will produce the results we want? Because we have clear goals that are measurable, quantifiable, and attainable. We will reach our goals because we are open to change, and we will continue to try new strategies and new programs until we find what works best. We have restructured, but we don't believe structure is as important as goals and a willingness to stick with those goals. Some of what we are doing may not work, but we cannot know that until we try. If we were not open to change, and if we had not already received good feedback about the new things we are doing, I might not be so confident.

Another positive factor is that our people don't give up. Although we are still declining in traditional indicators and our financial situation is bleak, our people don't give up. We have to keep trying. What alternative do we have? When we get our programs in order and begin meeting our goals, we will no longer have financial problems.

You won't hear gloom and doom here. Our people are future-oriented and optimistic. Their attitudes are positive.

Let me tell you some of the new things I have already done: First, I visited every person. That took a lot of time, but the people appreciated my caring enough to do that. They also appreciated that I shared my vision for the organization with them so they would know where we were going and what we were going to do.

Second, I took charge immediately. It was clear to me that people needed strong leadership to be confident in the future. I saw some things that could be changed for the better, so I acted quickly. Although a few people didn't like the changes, those who are forward-looking were appreciative.

Next, I moved people who had been in leadership for a long time out of their positions so we could have new blood and new ideas. Of course, those people who lost their positions weren't thrilled, but they are adjusting. I think they are happier now not to have so much to do. Fortunately, nobody left the organization. I think that says something about our people.

I also clarified job descriptions with each person. All people have specific jobs to do. If they all do them, everything will be covered. We will reach our goals. We say over and over, "Just do your job!" When everybody tries to do everything, all we get is confusion.

I helped our people see that our hard times are not entirely our fault. The world is changing. When everything is in transition, you have to wait to see what will happen. You have to be patient. Our organization is not the only one facing hard times. Look at the rest of the culture and at other organizations like ours.

I have tried to act swiftly when problems have arisen to decide what caused them so that we can keep them from happening again. We know that every problem has a cause, and that if we wait too long to find the cause, we may never find it. When we find the cause, we take steps to show the person who fouled up what not to do and how to watch carefully for this particular problem in the future. We find that if we help people see what not to do as well as what we want them to do, they make fewer mistakes.

Some people are slow to act. They remember how things were done in the "good old days." They like to analyze how things have changed. In the end, they usually decide that everything has changed for the worse. I don't know which is worse — the people who want to change everything or the people who never want to change anything.

I have been working harder at learning from people who are older and wiser — people with more experience. Whether in our organization or in others, there are always people who have learned by doing, and they have much to teach us. Learning from people who learned the hard way is the best kind of learning.

I also have emphasized teamwork and joint decision making. We bring leaders together to talk, coordinate, and make joint management decisions. People love working together, and we rarely get disruptive disagreements. That is because we have good people.

Finally, I brought in programs that I had used in other places. That gave us more variety. Yes, things are beginning to move here. If we stay with it, we will be successful.

Leadership as described above is defined by intentions and activities rather than by results, quality of output, and the ability to improve continually. We know that the activities instituted by the "leader" above are counterproductive and work against long-term systemic change and organizational improvement. Different assumptions about leadership have proven to be more productive. These include the following:

1. Being offered and placed in a position of leadership does not mean one can lead.
2. People searching for a leader do not necessarily find one.
3. A person who has held leadership positions over time has not automatically learned how to lead.
4. Organizations are as likely to choose leaders for the wrong reasons as for the right ones.
5. Leaders who postpone leading until they know all the people and all about the organization rarely get around to leading.
6. The opposite is true also: Persons who "take charge" before they know the organization tend to substitute activity, if not autocracy, for leadership.
7. Doing good things, even to bring about change, does not in itself move the organization forward.

8. Assuming that certain people do want change or that certain people do not want change is unfair and unhelpful.

9. Having clear and attainable goals — and even reaching them — does not mean that an organization is well led. The goals may be inappropriate.

10. Being willing to try new things until you find something that works will most often produce "sound and fury" rather than sound plans and strategies.

11. There is a thin line between optimism and apathy. Failing to give up on systems that fail to work may get in the way of designing systems that do work.

12. Visions come from the people. Leaders who too quickly state their own visions for an organization may work against people's dreaming and sharing of visions.

13. Taking charge in order to show one's strength is more likely to alienate people than to mobilize them.

14. Knowledge is more important than experience. Substitute training for perpetuating "the way we do it."

15. Leaders help people move out of narrow identification with their present positions to ownership of the larger organization and its shared vision.

16. Blaming other people, structures, or trends for problems does not motivate. The more usual result is frustration or apathy.

17. Focusing on simple cause-and-effect relationships is short-term thinking that hides understanding how long-term desired results are actually achieved.

18. It is important to see that many systems are designed slowly by attrition or evolution, eventuating in systems that are unable to produce even the results of an earlier time. The system looks the same, but its processes do not operate in the same way.

19. Teamwork is desirable when members are drawn by shared dreams and shared ownership of processes. "Teamwork" for coordination when people identify primarily with their individual positions is a sham and a waste of time.

Leadership seems tricky. It seems that one can defend almost any assumption. The reality is that leadership is difficult and complex, but not tricky.

It is possible to learn from people who have carefully studied leadership in our culture to construct theories and practices of leadership that are helpful, understandable, and workable.

It is possible to do that in the church. By and large, it has not been done in The United Methodist Church or in mainline Protestantism. Those leadership styles that are generally lifted up as models are for the most part individualistic, entrepreneurial, and not usable beyond the experience of the persons developing them.

> Leadership styles that are generally lifted up as models are for the most part individualistic, entrepreneurial, and not usable beyond the experience of the persons developing them.

Leadership is an art, and a science. Leadership is listening to the people of an organization to hear their deepest yearnings. It is stating a vision for the whole organization that comes out of and builds on those yearnings and on the organization's mission. Leadership is designing systems to achieve a shared vision. Leadership is managing the system to achieve the shared vision.

The first critical question of leadership is whether the leader has the ability to listen to people and to state their shared vision.

The second critical question of leadership is whether the leader can hold the vision, while at the same time designing and constructing a system to give life to the vision.

The third critical question of leadership is determining how much change the leader can lead in a given time and setting. Stating the vision and putting in place an appropriate system opens the door to the possibility of change. The change must be led and managed. An artist who turns the painting over to someone else or who tries to rely on the work of another artist will not produce a masterpiece.

The final critical question of leadership is whether the leader is willing to change him or herself. He or she must be willing to:

- ◆ Measure long-term results.
- ◆ Evaluate movement from the place of beginning to the desired end.
- ◆ Adjust the system.
- ◆ Change the way the system is managed.
- ◆ Recognize errors in leadership.
- ◆ Admit using leadership styles that were sometimes inappropriate or harmful and realize that new and different conduct may be expected.

Significant here is the leader's ability to call for radical change at times, to show that the most radical change may be required of the very person calling for change, and to make that change with a commitment to improvement. The leader does not need to feel shame or guilt. He or she needs only to acknowledge humanness, a measure of selflessness, and a passion for achieving the vision.

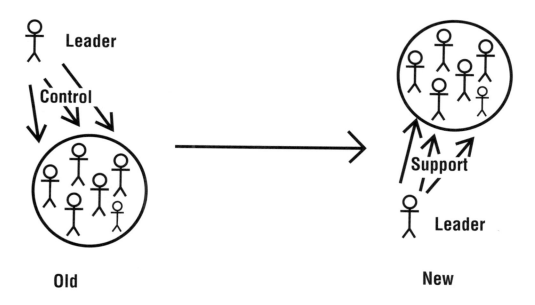

In the church today, we want to change to improve our ministry — our sharing of the gospel and our living the gospel. It is one thing for leaders to call for change and to attempt to direct the change. It is another thing for leaders to see that the primary change that is called for is a change in themselves, in the systems they lead, and in the ways they lead. The change in the leader becomes a declaration of the seriousness of the mission, the significance of the vision, and the kind of radical measures that are necessary to achieve it.

We don't like to change. We fear defeat or failure. It is difficult for us to see that everybody knows the present system is not working or not working well, and that our leadership is being called into question subtly or outside our presence. We blame other people, call for change in others, pile on ideas and suggestions from others and turn them into programs and activity, or we deny that the system is not working. We pursue whatever we can to avoid change.

Imagine a bishop in an annual conference, a pastor in a church, a general secretary in a general church agency, or a Sunday school teacher in a class announcing, "It is not working, but I can do something to improve the situation. I am changing what I do and how I do it. I will seek new knowledge, skills, and methods. You may hold me accountable as your leader for better results. I invite you to go with me into a world of new possibilities. I cannot do it all, but I will do what I can do, and I will help empower all participants to do that too. I invite you to follow a *new leader*!"

> *Quality in the church is achieved by improving the church's ministry. Achieving quality involves clarifying the church's aim, rebuilding and improving the ministry system, and managing the system to attain the aim.*

CHAPTER 9
The Ministry System

Ministry is people assisting people in Christian faith development. Ministry doesn't happen just in the church, but it does happen in the church and *through the auspices* of the church. Ministry is the reason the church exists.

Ministry is people offering Christ to one another and serving Christ and one another. In the church, ministry is accomplished through worship, the church school, special groups, the sacraments, and much more. Everything the church is and does is a system that delivers ministry.

Local churches have varying degrees of quality of ministry. The differences are due to:

- The local church's clarity about its aim.
- The ability of the congregation's system to deliver that aim.
- The capability of the leader of the congregation to state the aim, align all participants around it, and put in place and manage a system to deliver that aim.

Quality in the church is achieved by improving the church's ministry. Achieving quality involves clarifying the church's aim, rebuilding and improving the ministry system, and managing the system to attain the aim.

Quality in the church is improving ministry to such a degree that it delights those who come. Quality is delivering ministry consistently with little variation in the quality, and it is having a system capable of continually improving ministry.

Quality in ministry is reaching out to people with neighborly caring. It is helping people find community and find God in that community. Quality is enabling people to love God as disciples of Jesus Christ. Quality in ministry is living every day as loving, forgiving people.

Even quality ministry can be improved by working on the core process of the church and continually checking at critical places where critical components come together. These places are the "Core Improvement Points" (CIPs).

The following ministry diagram shows four major components of ministry: (1) the people coming; (2) the congregation; (3) the pastor or leader; (4) the people departing.

The Ministry System

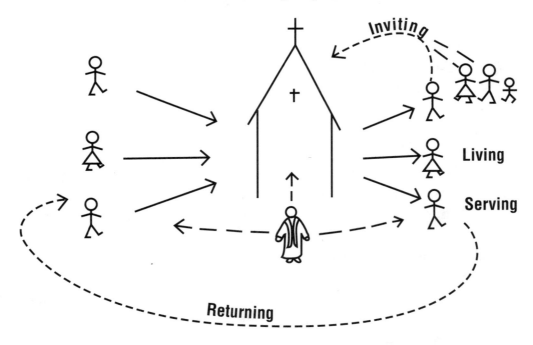

The CIPs are these components and the relationships among these components. The "Core Improvement Points" in the diagram are:

(1) People coming to church and bringing new people with them.
(2) People being received with care and love by the congregation.
(3) Life in the congregation that builds faith and relates people to God.
(4) People transformed in the church, going out to live new lives.
(5) People extending the church, living as Christ's disciples.
(6) The pastor — called, trained, knowledgeable — facilitating the work of ministry for all the people.
(7) The pastor preparing the people of the church to reach out and receive others.
(8) The pastor carefully leading the people in building, managing, and continually improving the processes of congregational life.
(9) The pastor and people going out together to make the world more loving and just.
(10) People returning to church and bringing new people with them.

The Ministry System

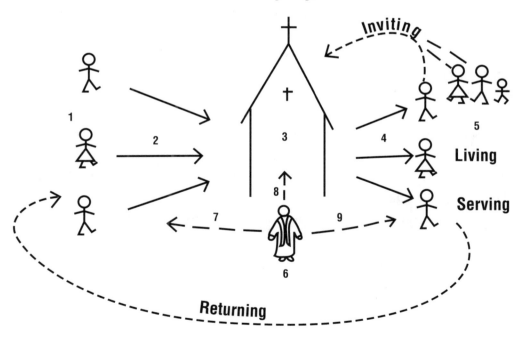

When these ten "Core Improvement Points" are functioning well, the system is in control. It is stable. It is producing the aim intended with little variation. As the system is regularly checked and improved, so is the ministry. Public relations and marketing are done spontaneously and enthusiastically by word of mouth, by eager invitations, and by stories of delight.

If the "Core Improvement Points" are not functioning well, the ministry system may be out of control. Such a system is unstable and unpredictable. It is difficult to know what the system will produce or if it will produce at all. Quality ministry in this situation is tenuous.

The only way to achieve quality through an unstable system is to work to improve major processes that contribute to the core process. The solution is to rebuild the system one component and one relationship at a time.

For continuing quality of ministry, there must be continual evaluating, testing, renewing, and changing. The pastor must manage this process, which must come out of the vision of the people and move toward that vision.

The vision and aim will be formed out of people's personal hopes and their hopes for their community. When the church provides quality ministry, the whole community will be a better place.

The ministry system, as we have described it, is simple and basic. It affects all the church is and does, the lives of all who participate, and the lives of all who relate to those who participate. The results are far-reaching. Congregations that concentrate on improving the ministry system are able to reach far beyond the system to add offerings of outreach and service.

When a local church has a problem, its leaders should check first the processes of the basic system. They can't ignore these or go around them. Better still, leaders are well advised to work every day to improve the system. The chances are that there will not be as many problems.

*Financial giving is intricately related to the basic
ministry system of the church. People come to
church, are served and serve, and are transformed.
As a part of serving, they give a portion of their
financial assets to the church.*

*Giving is an act of institutional support and an act
of thanksgiving and dedication. It is a spiritual
discipline and a response to grace.*

> *The leaders of The United Methodist Church can design and construct a well-functioning financial system in the denomination even as they lead the church to improve or rebuild its total ministry system.*

CHAPTER 10
Financial Giving

Systems, by definition, are all-inclusive. Every part is related in some way to every other part. A systems approach to the church — such as Quest for Quality — allows and even demands that funding the church's ministry be seen as an integral component of the ministry system.

Financial giving begins in the congregation, but extends far beyond that single body. Besides local church ministries, the funds raised support conference administration and programs, schools, homes, hospitals, camps, conference centers, general church agencies, colleges and seminaries, and worldwide mission efforts.

Numerous factors affect giving to the church, including:

1. People's overall feeling about the value of the church in their lives.
2. People's perception about the role of the church in their faith growth and spiritual formation.

3. How well the primary task — reaching out, receiving, relating, nurturing, and sending — is functioning in the church.
4. The level of family and/or primary group commitment to the church.
5. The presence and compelling quality of the vision of the church.
6. Programming around core processes of ministry that target people in relation to their needs and interests.
7. The quality of pastoral leadership in the congregation and the pastor's attitudes about money.
8. The sense that the congregation is administered for people.
9. The inclination of church leaders to listen to people and to use the information gathered to improve the church's ministry.

The complexity of the financial system in The United Methodist Church is staggering. There are more than 35,000 congregations in the United States. Each one serves a different community or region, and each has different attitudes and values about money and giving.

Financial giving is intricately related to the basic ministry system of the church. People come to church, are served and serve, and are transformed. As a part of serving, they give a portion of their financial assets to the church. Giving is an act of institutional support and an act of thanksgiving and dedication. It is a spiritual discipline and a response to grace.

The tendency in the church is to oversimplify the financial giving system because:

♦ The complexity of the whole system can easily lead to inaction.
♦ No one person or group controls more than a few processes.
♦ It is difficult to know appropriate points for initial intervention.
♦ People tend to believe that it is better to do something than to do nothing.

Quality Improvement theory has taught us, however, that "doing something" is not necessarily better than "doing nothing." We may make matters worse by tampering with the system.

We may make matters worse by tampering with the system.

We cannot afford to:

◆ Blame people.
◆ Generally increase marketing efforts.
◆ Selectively increase training or information dissemination.
◆ Call people together in pep rallies.
◆ Send out pleas for institutional loyalty.
◆ Reduce spending and assume we have dealt with income issues.

None of the above actions will improve the system of financial giving in the church. They constitute tampering with the system, not basic system improvement.

There is an alternative: Through understanding systems and quality leadership, we can intervene to initiate change and continue that change until core systems and primary processes are in good working order. We can then continue improvement efforts by working to improve or rebuild processes that support, extend, and enhance the core processes of financial giving.

Within The United Methodist Church, the bishops are one group of leaders who can initiate the renewal of the financial and ministry systems of the church. What is done will depend on the circumstances in each conference. In some conferences, the financial system is in serious disarray. Other conferences need only give careful attention to strengthen one or more basic processes.

The church's financial system was designed for the results it is getting. Pushing the system harder will not cause it to produce substantially better results. If better results are desired and are possible, the leaders of the church will have to lead the way in designing and installing a new system or a renewed system. The task cannot be delegated to others within the system or to experts outside the system. Such people can help, but only the *leaders* can change the direction of an organization.

What we need in The United Methodist Church is:

◆ Knowledge about our financial system — how it works and how to improve it and repair it.
◆ The ability to predict what the system can do and will do in a stable environment.

♦ Understanding about how financial giving and financial management are appropriately related.

The leaders of The United Methodist Church can design and construct a well-functioning financial system in the denomination even as they lead the church to improve or rebuild its total ministry system. We instinctively know the systems are interrelated. The task is to understand and redesign them.

Congregational Ministry

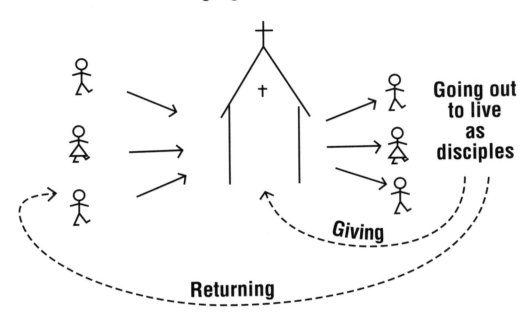

The basic pattern of participation in the church is that people come in, are related to God and nurtured in the faith, and return to the world. As they go out, people extend the church. Periodically they return and contribute their time and/or money to support the church.

In The United Methodist Church:

♦ Some funds are spent locally;
♦ Other funds are sent to the conference;
♦ Some funds are spent by the conference;
♦ Other funds are sent to support the general church;
♦ Some funds are spent to support general church structures and ministries;
♦ Other funds are sent to support ministries beyond the denomination.

UMC Financial Giving System

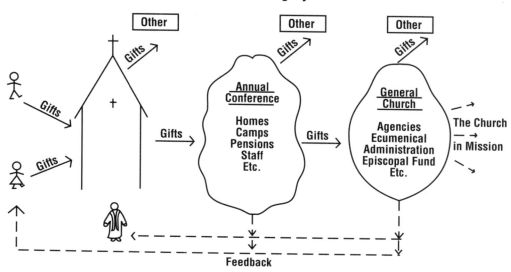

Completing the funding cycle is feedback. The general church reports to the conference, the pastor, the congregation, and directly to church members about the use of funds. The conference also provides feedback to the congregation. The people who give through their local churches participate in extended ministry across the world. Information coming back to them nurtures their sense of discipleship and produces ownership of the church's larger ministry.

The normal cycle of giving and feedback may be disrupted at any one of many critical points in the system. However, the cycle may be improved at those same points — the "Core Improvement Points." Some of the primary points are:

◆ The love and care with which people are welcomed and assimilated in the church.
◆ Training in financial giving as a part of new member orientation.
◆ The quality of the church's ministry through worship, nurture, service, and fellowship.
◆ Expectations and accountability structures that elicit commitment to Christian living and support of the church and the church's larger mission.
◆ The pastor's attitudes about money and knowledge of and commitment to the church's institutional needs and outreach.

- Use of funds by the conference, the general church, and beyond the denomination.
- Adequate feedback from the general church and annual conference.
- Does feedback about the use of funds please the original giver? Does it build trust, or does it foster mistrust and suspicion?
- Are the positive stories of people being served strong enough to counter false information, distrust, or controversy?

The above points are just a few that could be targeted to help improve the total financial system of the church.

Let's return again to the relationship between the basic ministry system and financial giving. When the primary task of ministry is working well in the congregation, people respond. The most important factor in the level of functioning of the primary task of ministry in the congregation is the ability and willingness of the pastor to lead. That factor is at the heart of the primary task of the annual conference. Perhaps the most significant thing the annual conference could do to improve financial giving would be to work on the core process of leader development.

> When the primary task of ministry is working well in the congregation, people respond.

Would annual conferences have financial problems if the core process were working effectively in every congregation? No. Strengthening the core process is the most important factor for bringing about long-term financial strength. Other components will need work, but they cannot substitute for the basics.

The general church also needs attention. Our failure to listen to givers and the will of the whole church is a toxin in the church system that is destroying the strength of our connection and the efficacy of our ministry. Budgeting processes at the general level of the church must not ignore one group of people at the expense of another. The general church system as it stands today is not responsive or flexible. It is a system attacked by many, and defended by few. All the while, the financial system grows weaker and more unpredictable.

Perhaps the weakest part of the financial system at the general church and every level is communication or interpretation. We attempt advertising and fund raising rather than connecting people in ministry at the level of their deepest desires to be good disciples. Giving people more information when they want to be personally involved in ministry is ineffective and offensive.

A 1990 study commissioned by United Methodist Communications found a growing distrust of centralized authority and programs, a lack of knowledge of the church's benevolence funds, poor use of promotional materials by local churches, and clergy with little training in interpreting the church structure.

Simply providing more information will not clear up mistrust and misunderstandings. Until we address major ministry and discipleship processes, we will simply be tampering with the system.

> Simply providing more information will not clear up mistrust and misunderstandings.

We must have a leader for this task — someone who has the authority to design and improve basic systems and manage the many processes for improvement. As with all United Methodist systems, the leadership must be initiated at the annual conference level. The bishop and cabinet, working with other persons who own the financial processes, can start and lead improvement efforts. They cannot delegate it or turn the responsibility over to the Council on Finance and Administration. From the conference, improvement actions can extend through the General Conference to the general church and through the pastors and lay members of the annual conference to each congregation.

The biggest block to serious, substantive, and sustained improvement of the United Methodist financial giving system is the seeming inability of conference cabinets to see beyond quick fixes to pay attention to the core processes of basic ministry, congregational leadership, and getting good data about why people give to the church. Rebuilding and improving these major processes would open the possibility of simplifying a system that has become multilayered and overburdened. This would also provide an opening to re-envision our mission and develop leaders who would make the vision real in the churches.

Blaming people does not repair the system. The system currently in place does all it can do. It cries out for improvement in basic processes. We must improve the system.

> Blaming people does not repair the system.

In summary, the primary questions before us are:

- How can we understand the total financial giving system of The United Methodist Church?
- What are the primary points or processes where the system can break down and thus be improved?
- Who can give leadership to improve the system?
- Where are the primary points of entry for working on the system?
- Who should make decisions about the church's finances?
- What is the core process of the church's system of finances?
- How long will it be before we move from short-term fund-raising to long-term financial giving grounded in the church's primary task?

The vision comes from the people and, once stated, can be shared through processes that allow all the people to affirm and own it. The vision must be stated by someone who has the authority to state it.

John Wesley stated a vision for the Methodist societies: "To redeem the nation; to spread Scriptural holiness throughout the land."

> *Most United Methodists have the seeds of two complementary visions . . . One is a vision of knowing and loving God and knowing that God knows and loves them. The other is that their church will be a dynamic, growing, Spirit-filled institution where they will find Christian community in a positive, hope-filled setting.*

EPILOGUE
Who Will State the Vision?

A vision is an image of something in the future. A vision may be personal, or it may be shared, such as the image a young married couple have of their life together. A family, a business, or any organization may share a common vision so powerful that it captures the members' imagination and allegiance and pulls them toward it.

For members of an organization to share a vision, someone — the leader — must listen to their deepest yearnings and then state a common vision. The first and most important responsibility of a leader is to state the vision for the group. The vision comes from the people and, once stated, can be shared through processes that allow all the people to affirm and own it. The vision must be stated by someone who has the authority to state it. Once stated, the vision can be heard, considered, and ultimately owned and honored by the people.

Who will state the vision for The United Methodist Church of the twenty-first century? Who will state the vision now so that the whole church can hear and embrace it before the new century dawns? Who will state a vision that is connected to the past, but directed toward the future?

Who will state a balanced vision? A vision that is already in the hearts of people?

Who has the position and authority to state the vision? Who has access to our dreams, hopes, and trust?

At present, the answer is unclear. Pastors can state the vision for their congregations, but their visions must participate in the shared vision of the annual conference. A Sunday school teacher can state a vision for a class, but that vision cannot be divorced from the vision of the whole congregation. Similarly, a conference's vision is tied to that of the whole denomination.

The General Conference has responsibility for clarifying our theology and indicating direction for the church, but this body of one thousand people cannot state the vision for the church. The General Conference can contribute to the vision and share in it once it is stated, but this body cannot give it voice with clarity and power.

Who will state the vision for The United Methodist Church? Two hundred fifty years ago, John Wesley stated a vision for the Methodist societies. It was simple, clear, and powerful. In his words, the vision was "to redeem the nation; to spread Scriptural holiness throughout the land."

Wesley's vision had the power to guide the Methodist movement for at least a century. In America, particularly, the vision was realized, as Methodism became the largest Protestant denomination and the most widely dispersed religious organization in the nation.

As pointed out earlier, in the latter half of the nineteenth century, the fortunes of The Methodist Church began to wane. For the first time since it began in America, the denomination began to trail total population growth. For well over a century, the Methodist Church has failed to hold its penetration level in the population. Although actual decreases in Methodist membership did not begin until the mid-1960s, the factors leading up to the decline began in the previous century.

Wesley stated the vision for the church during its first century. Others have done it since his time, and they are still revered in all parts of the church. Their visions were about . . .

ECUMENISM AND THE ONENESS OF THE CHURCH —
   John R. Mott, Philip Potter, Charles Parlin.
DEVELOPING CHURCHES AND CARING FOR THE PIONEERS WHO PUSHED THE
   U.S. FRONTIERS WESTWARD —
   Frances Asbury, Philip Embury, Philip Otterbein, Jacob Albright, Harry Hoosier.
ESTABLISHING JUSTICE AND SOCIAL HOLINESS —
   *Thelma Stevens, Bromley Oxnam, Barbara Heck, Frances Willard,
   Georgia Harkness.*
HIGHER EDUCATION FOR ALL PEOPLE —
   *Gordon Gould, James Thomas, Emilio de Carvalho, John Stewart,
   Belle Harris Bennett.*
TAKING THE GOSPEL TO THE ENDS OF THE EARTH —
   William Taylor, Adam Clark, Jason Lee, Tracy Jones, E. Stanley Jones.
SPIRITUAL FORMATION —
   Fletcher Mandalay, Grover Emmons, Rueben Job.
EVANGELISM —
   Harry Denman.
EMERGENCY RELIEF FOR PEOPLE IN CRISIS —
   Lynn Harold Huff, Harry Haines.

Think about other church leaders who have been visionary and who have rallied large followings for great causes . . .

PAUL OF TARSUS *and the first great missionary movement of Christianity in the
   first century, A.D.*
MARTIN LUTHER *and the Protestant Reformation in the sixteenth century.*
MARTIN LUTHER KING, JR. *and the American Civil Rights Movement of the
   1950s and 1960s.*

The question remains, *"Who will state the vision in our time for The United Methodist Church in the twenty-first century?"* What will be the person's source of authority? How will he or she listen to our people to hear the vision that God is already planting there? What position in the church will he or she hold? Who can state the vision for the whole church?

Perhaps in The United Methodist Church the vision can be stated initially in the annual conference. If so, who can state it there? Who *will* state it there?

Once the vision for the larger connection is stated, who will state it in the congregations? Who will make it real for the people who seek God in the church and those who help one another live lives of neighborly caring?

Most United Methodists seem to have the seeds of two complementary visions in their hearts: One is a vision of knowing and loving God and knowing that God knows and loves them. The other is the vision that their church will be a dynamic, growing, Spirit-filled institution where they will find Christian community in a positive, hope-filled setting.

The vision for the church must be stated by people who are leaders in the mainline of ministry in the church — people who lead congregations and annual conferences. Leaders do not have to be the greatest visionaries themselves. The vision may come from anyone. The leaders do have to state the vision, however. Leaders also have to keep the vision before the people and remind them of the progress that is being made to achieve the vision. Otherwise, the people might assume that they are failing and give up. If people are moving toward the vision, it will be because the leader has helped the people build a system for doing that and is managing the system to move toward the vision.

Visionary aim, a system to reach the aim, and leadership are the three basic components of quality improvement. All three rely upon the first leadership task — stating the vision.

> Visionary aim, a system to reach the aim, and leadership are the three basic components of quality improvement.

Who will state the vision for The United Methodist Church? Who will put in place a system capable of producing such a vision?

A front page article in *The New York Times*, Sunday, September 6, 1992, discussed President Bush's difficulty in convincing the American public that they should vote him a second term in office. One notable sentence read, "One of the reasons George Bush is in trouble is that his image now is of wanting to be President more than of wanting to accomplish things as President."

One sometimes gets the impression in the church that people will spend much more energy to achieve a high place of leadership than they will to accomplish the task of leading once they get there. Regarding leaders in the church who may have guaranteed appointments or life tenure, it may be hard for the people to predict whether getting to be a leader or actually leading is the primary driving force.

It is most probable that a vision for the church will be stated first in one annual conference; then in a second. Others will follow when they see the power of a vision to pull people to its reality. The vision will then move through congregations and church agencies as the whole system comes on board.

If you have ever participated in an organization or group that had purpose and expectation, widespread commitment and ownership, leadership setting direction and calling out of the people their deepest longings and their best contributions, you know the joy and fulfillment that such an experience can bring. Being part of a community that is vision-driven is an unforgettable experience. It happens in youth groups, political campaigns, and work relationships. It happens on football teams, in the band, in fraternities and sororities. It happened in the civil rights movement and in the women's movement. It can happen anywhere. It happened before in United Methodism. It can happen again.

> Being part of a community that is vision-driven is an unforgettable experience.

One of the most powerful hindrances for a vision being spawned, stated, shared, and practiced in our church is the pervasive and growing belief among both laity and clergy that only congregational life counts any more in United Methodism. Each congregation, if it looks for a vision at all, looks for one that is only big enough for itself. The conference is ignored.

There seems to be good reason for this. There are some people in The United Methodist Church who are stating visions for their congregations. On the other hand, where are the people who know how to lead annual conferences? What conference leaders are stating visions that come out of the hearts of the people rather than out of the needs of the institution?

The nature of denominationalism is changing. The new birth will be at the heart of a vision that is able to steer The United Methodist Church into the future. May God help us to state a vision worthy of our whole church.

The first question is, *"Who will state the vision?*

The second question is, *"When?"*

Suggested Readings

James D. Anderson and Ezra Earl Jones. *The Management of Ministry: Leadership, Purpose, Structure, Community.* San Francisco: Harper and Row, 1978.

Joel Arthur Barker. *Future Edge: Discovering New Paradigms of Success.* New York: William Morrow & Company, Inc., 1992.

W. Edwards Deming. *The New Economics.* Cambridge, Massachusetts: Massachusetts Institute of Technology: Center for Advanced Engineering Study, 1993.

W. Edwards Deming. *Out of the Crisis.* Cambridge, Massachusetts: Massachusetts Institute of Technology: Center for Advanced Engineering Study, 1986.

Peter Senge. *The Fifth Discipline: The Art and Practice of the Learning Organization.* New York: Doubleday/Currency, 1990.

Mary Walton. *The Deming Management Method.* New York: Perigee Books/The Putnam Publishing Group, 1986.